VICTORIA & ALBERT MUSEUM

# ARMS AND ARMOUR OF OLD JAPAN

BY

B. W. ROBINSON

*LONDON*

HER MAJESTY'S STATIONERY OFFICE

ILLUSTRATED BOOKLET NO. 6



*First published 1951*

*Fifth impression 1983*

ISBN 0 11 290074 7

COVER ILLUSTRATION: Utagawa Kuniyoshi (1797–1861)
The warrior Negoro no Komizucha amid a hail of weapons,
from the series *Taiheiki Yeiyūden*.
Signed *Ichiyūsai Kuniyoshi ga* 1847–1850. E 10799–1886

# ARMS AND ARMOUR OF OLD JAPAN

It has always been upon arms and armour that the craftsmen of Japan have lavished their choicest workmanship. The Japanese sword-blade is proverbial for strength and sharpness, and whilst in many countries the sword has been highly regarded and richly adorned, the spiritual and symbolic qualities with which the Japanese blade has always been invested in the country of its origin, as well as its beauty of form and its terrible effectiveness, make it unique among the weapons of mankind. It was therefore natural that the highest craftsmanship and the most tireless skill should be employed in the making of all its mounts and accessories.

It was the Japanese sword too which largely dictated the peculiar form and construction of Japanese armour. To western eyes the latter may appear at once clumsy in design and frail in texture; but the innumerable overlapping strips of steel, iron, and toughened cow-hide of which it is composed, firmly and closely laced with silk or leather, give it the maximum lightness and flexibility, and constitute the only effective protection against the two-handed stroke of a Japanese sword.

## BLADES

The Japanese sword has a legendary origin in the remote and fabulous Age of the Gods, but it has a well-cherished and continuous historical tradition from the beginning of the VIIIth century. It was during the period Taihō (701–704) that Amakuni, the first of the twelve thousand odd Japanese swordsmiths whose names and dates are known to us, is said to have made and signed a few blades of high quality which were the prototypes of the weapons here illustrated. A century or more later was born Yasutsuna who worked, we are assured, under divine inspiration, and in whose hands the Japanese sword-blade became firmly established in the form it has retained ever since. Thus a Japanese blade never went out of date, as did the constantly changing swords of Europe, and this important fact made it possible for a Japanese officer of the XXth century to carry and use on the battlefield the same weapon which his ancestors had wielded perhaps six or seven centuries before.

After the foundations had been laid by Amakuni and Yasutsuna, the next important period of activity and development came towards the end of the Xth century, and under the Emperor Ichijō (987–1012) flourished, among many notable swordsmiths, the great Munechika of Kyōto (see plate 4), Tomonari of Bizen, and Masakuni of Satsuma, all of whom founded schools whose traditions descended unbroken down to the XIXth century and later.

The civil wars of the late XIIth century gave another great fillip to the craft, which culminated at the beginning of the next century when the retired Emperor Go-Toba became so fascinated with swords and sword-forging that he summoned the most eminent smiths in the country to attend him in rotation, demonstrate their skill, and give him instruction. He himself forged blades of high quality, a few of which, marked on the tang with the imperial chrysanthemum (and hence called *kiku-go-saku*, or "honourable chrysanthemum make"), are treasured in Japan. To this memorable epoch belongs the foundation of several famous schools, the Senju-in of Yamato, the Awataguchi of Yamashiro, the Ichimonji of Bizen, and the Aoye of Bitchū, of which the greatest exponents were Yukinobu (*circa* 1130–1200), Hisakuni (1149–1216), Norimune (1159–1214), and Moritsugu (1106–1190) respectively.

The late XIIIth and early XIVth century, which includes the civil wars of Taiheiki, is the next great period of the swordsmith's craft—the greatest of all—when Yoshimitsu of Awataguchi (1229–1291), Masamune of Sagami (1264–1343), and the latter's most eminent pupil Gō Yoshihiro (1299–1325), authoritatively pronounced to be the three greatest swordsmiths who ever lived, were at work. In influence and prestige Masamune has the pre-eminence, and his forge at the feudal capital of Kamakura was the resort of eminent and ambitious swordsmiths from many outlying provinces, who spread his practice throughout the country on their return home. Of his pupils (apart from Yoshihiro, above) the most noteworthy were his adopted son Sadamune (1298–1349), Sa of Chikuzen (1277–1356), Kanemitsu of Bizen (1280–1358), and Kaneuji of Mino (1284–1344). Other celebrated smiths of this period were the centenarian Rai Kunitoshi (1240–1344) and the sinister Muramasa of Ise (b. 1341?) whose blades, though of the highest quality, bore a reputation for bloodthirstiness and ill-luck.

There were further periods of great activity, but less brilliance, round the years 1400 and 1500 when large numbers of blades were turned out particularly at Osafune, a small village in Bizen province populated almost entirely by swordsmiths. The prolonged civil wars of the XVIth century also created a large demand for blades which was met by the growing number of swordsmiths who were by now established in almost every province. A notable development of the XVIth century was the growing popularity of the type of blade made at Seki in Mino province; this was a shorter and stouter blade than the traditional type which had been designed for use on horseback. Fighting was now mostly on foot, to which the Seki blades, perfected by Kanemoto, were ideally suited.

From the welter of the XVIth century Tokugawa Iyeyasu finally emerged supreme, and Japan entered upon two and a half centuries of peace and seclusion. Japanese authorities have made this the great break in the history of their national weapon, blades produced before 1600 being designated *kotō*, or "old swords", and those made subsequently *shintō* ("new swords"), though of late the term *kinkotō* ("near-old swords") has been substituted for the latter. In spite of the peaceful conditions prevailing, the XVIIth century was a great period of the swordsmith's craft, with peaks occurring about the years 1615 and 1675. With the first of these peaks are associated the names of Umetada Myōju (1558–1632) who derived his descent from Munechika, and Horikawa Kunihiro (1539–1614) of Kyōto, Tadayoshi (1572–1632) of Hizen, and Hankei (d. 1646) of Yedo. By 1675 most of the best blades were being produced at Ōsaka by Tsuta Sukehiro (1635–1682), his pupil Sukenao, and Inouye Shinkai (d. 1682), but the blades of their contemporary Kotetsu Okisato of Yedo (1599–1678) are second to none during the *shintō* period.

The XVIIIth century was a time of stagnation and decline until, towards its close, the blades of Suishinshi Masahide (1750–1825) began to appear. He was the moving spirit in a great revival of the craft, and went back to the *kotō* period for his models, forging chiefly in the old styles of Bizen and Sagami; and by writing several excellent books embodying his principles, exerted an enormous influence on his contemporaries and successors. Of the former the most noteworthy were Masayoshi (1731–1819) and Motohira (1742–1827) of Satsuma, and of the latter, his pupils Naotane (1779–1857) and Naokatsu (1805–1858), and Kiyomaro "the Masamune of Yotsuya". This period is known as the *shinshintō* ("very new sword") or, by those who use "*kinkotō*" for the preceding epoch, the *shintō* period.

In 1877 came the imperial edict abolishing the wearing of swords; strange to say, it was obeyed with hardly a murmur. This was a very severe blow to the swordsmith's craft, and almost the only blades produced from that time until the recent war were for official presentation or dedication in temples. The old traditions were kept alive, however, and a few of the blades made for Japanese officers serving in that war would bear comparison with the best of any period. The majority, however, were mass-produced in imitation of the Seki style which, as has been already noted, was considered the most suitable for use by infantry.

The reason for the exceptional strength and sharpness of the Japanese blade is that it was composed of a soft iron core enclosed by harder metal, the edge of which was separately tempered to an extreme hardness. The blade would thus take an edge like a razor whilst the composition of the "body" of it ensured toughness and a certain resilience. There is no space here to describe the whole forging and tempering process, which was lengthy and intricate, varying considerably between different schools, periods, and even individual swordsmiths. But the most obvious outward signs of these variations are the depth and outline of the specially tempered edge, which can be clearly seen in plates 10–13, and the different patterns of the graining or "damask" which appears on the surface of the metal between the tempered edge and the central ridge. These characteristic features, together with the general shape and proportions of the blade, are the most important among the many which a Japanese connoisseur will consider in assigning any given blade to its correct school and period.

Blades for spears, glaives (*naginata*), and arrows were often made and sometimes signed by well-known swordsmiths. Some fine examples are illustrated on plate 23, but as a rule these are not of as high a quality as the blades of swords and dirks.

## SWORD-FURNITURE

As has already been stressed, the high regard in which the Japanese held their sword-blades ensured that they should be superbly mounted and adorned. The Japanese are probably the only nation in the world whose men-folk were debarred by the custom of over a thousand years from the use of what we describe as jewellery. But from the XVth century onwards at least, they found an outlet for the gratification of personal vanity and the display of wealth in the decoration of the various types of sword and dagger whose wear was regulated by the strictest of etiquette and to a great extent by the law of the land. The use of gems or semi-precious stones, however, found no favour among them, unless it were in certain types of sword reserved for the highest nobility at the Imperial Court. It is indeed exceptional to find anything but metal employed for the more decorative of the mounts which served both to strengthen and to adorn the sword at various points.

In the period which concerns us here the Japanese *samurai* always carried his swords in pairs. When he wore armour, a long sword (*tachi*) hung suspended at his left side, and a short dirk (*tantō*) was thrust through his girdle; but when in civilian dress he wore a long sword (*katana*) and "companion-sword" (*wakizashi*) both carried edge uppermost in the girdle. The *tachi* tended to be longer than the *katana*, while the *tantō* was shorter than the *wakizashi*. The great majority of Japanese swords are mounted for civilian wear, and it was upon them that the skilled metalworkers found the widest scope for the exercise of their craft.

The mounts of a civilian sword consisted of:

(i) the guard (*tsuba*), which is as a rule flat and comparatively thin; very thick guards and "cupped" or concave examples are the exception. In size it varies greatly, but its outline is always of a compact form.

(ii) the handle (*kodzuka*) of a small knife carried sometimes in the scabbard of the companion-sword. It varies but little in size, and is nearly always of regular oblong outline. One in the shape of a dried fish and another fashioned as a bridge-post exemplify exceptional forms.

(iii) a skewer-like implement (*kōgai*) carried on the other side of the scabbard exhibits even less variety of form. Occasionally it is made in two pieces (*wari-kōgai*), as if for use as "chop-sticks".

(iv) the pommel (*kashira*) and ferrule or collar (*fuchi*) at either end of the hilt.

(v) the pair of ornaments (*menuki*) under the silk hilt-binding on either side. These probably originated as ornamental ends of the peg which secures the blade in the hilt, and were also intended to improve the grip by fitting into the hollow of the hands.

(vi) the scabbard-mounts, which were usually confined to a slotted projection (*kurikata*) through which passed the silken cord securing the sword in the girdle, and the chape or butt-mount (*kojiri*).

The period of serious activity in the making of decorative sword-mounts may be reckoned roughly as the 450 years ending with the decree, already referred to, by which the wearing of swords was prohibited in 1877. Some three thousand craftsmen of note are recorded to have made sword-furniture during this period, and they may be grouped under more than sixty distinct schools, each with its individual style and technical qualities.

The earliest guards of the historic period appear to have been discs of plain lacquered leather rimmed with metal for strength, or else of undecorated iron. In the XVth century, it would seem, a certain amount of decoration was imported into the iron guard in the form of simple piercing or primitive inlay of brass and copper. About the same time the other mounts described above came into use and received decorative treatment of the same kind.

Towards 1500 the influence of Buddhist thought and idealism as propagated by the Zen sect gradually elevated the minor crafts, metal-working especially, to the dignity of the higher arts, besides increasing the estimation in which the sword itself was held. The artist was now proud to sign his work, and the execution of freer designs coupled with the inlaying or incrustation of the softer metals and alloys, as well as the production of exquisite surface-patinas on iron itself, made great strides from this time onwards.

After 1600 this development was greatly fostered by the lessening prospect of civil war and the growth of national prosperity under the settled Tokugawa government, but the way had already been led not only by the great armourers and swordsmiths, the Myōchin and the Umetada, with their bold hammer technique and their broad but sparing inlay as applied to sword-furniture, but particularly by the famous Gotō family, who worked for the Shogunal Court and originated the technique of fine relief-sculpture in gold on the favourite black alloy *shakudō*, with its "fishroe" surface (see plate 15). The influence of this family, of which as many as three hundred masters are recorded in direct affiliation, is only greater than that exerted by the Nara school. This school originated in Yedo in the latter half of the XVIIth century, breaking away from the somewhat rigid traditions of the Gotō, and enlisted in its service a more extensive palette of the coloured alloys, as well as a greater freedom in the choice of subjects, these being adapted chiefly from the more naturalistic designs of the Kano painters. Another school of far-reaching influence is that of the Yokoya. Founded towards 1650, it pursued the Gotō style until its third master, Sōmin, introduced an entirely new technique, that of engraving in imitation of brush-strokes, applied to designs taken largely from the Ukiyoye, or Popular School of drawing.

The remaining families or groups of workers will be found for the most part to display either a development or a mixture of the styles above-mentioned. Special attention must be drawn, however, to the foreign influences—Chinese, Korean, and even Portuguese and Dutch—exerted both in technique and in design upon the workers in the Namban ("southern barbarian" i.e. foreign) and enamelling styles of Hizen province and Yedo.

Decadence and over-elaboration became characteristic of much sword-furniture towards the middle of the XIXth century; but even this last period of decay is illuminated here and there by the brilliant work of Shummei Hōgen, Hata Nobuyoshi, Gotō Ichijō and his pupils, and Kano Natsuo who died as late as 1898.

## ARMOUR

Japanese armour of earlier date than the XVIth century is of great rarity. Even in Japan only sixty full suits of the earlier periods are preserved. But suits made up at comparatively late dates often include early parts. Thus the helmet-crown of the Akita armour, one of the finest armours in the Museum, is boldly certified as the work of an armourer of the late XIIth century, though the suit as it now stands was not made up until 1748.

The earliest forms of armour recovered from the dolmen burials in various parts of Japan appear to have been, first, a kind of brigandine of leather fastening in front, upon which plates of metal were laced, and secondly, a plated and riveted cuirass all of metal, skilfully fitted to the upper half of the body. Judging from clay figures found in the same burials, both forms seem to have been provided with a fairly wide protective skirt, probably of leather, reaching to the knee. The legs of these figures are enclosed in wide trousers. The helmets are well-formed, and fitted with ear-pieces and neck-protectors.

During the Vth–VIIth centuries increasing intercourse with the mainland introduced horses into Japan, and fighting on horseback became the rule, bows and arrows being extensively used. At the same time armour made of small plates, laced together and overlapping, was introduced, of which some fragments are preserved in the Imperial Repository of Shōsō-in at Nara, which date from the reign of the Emperor Shōmu (724–748), and a model or toy suit of the same type, said to have been made by a court-lady for Prince Shōtoku (572–621), is in the Imperial Household Treasury.

This was the form which the Japanese at length adopted, modifying it to suit their special requirements and improving in every way upon their continental models. This process proceeded apace during the Xth–XIIth centuries, a period which saw the rise of the great military families and the consequent civil wars, which resolved themselves during the later XIIth century into a sanguinary struggle between the Taira and Minamoto clans.

During this era were developed the two basic forms of Japanese armour as we know it. The "great harness" (*ōyoroi*) was worn by generals and warriors of high rank; it was complete with helmet and large shoulder- and arm-protectors, the latter taking the place of a shield, which was never carried by the Japanese of the historical period, both hands being required for the use of bow and arrow on horseback. The second type was called *haramaki* ("wrapping the belly"). It consisted mainly of cuirass and tassets and was worn by the common soldiers who dispensed with helmets and shoulder-pieces; it was thus much less elaborate in construction and more limited in the protection it afforded than the "great harness". Nevertheless it was far lighter and more flexible, being designed for use on foot, and since hand-to-hand fighting was on the increase towards the end of this period the *haramaki* gained in popularity.

The XIIIth and XIVth centuries are generally known as the Kamakura period, that being the name of the town where the successive Shōguns, or supreme military governors, established their capital. The old imperial capital of Kyōto and the Emperor himself and his court relapsed into comparative insignificance. It was a golden era for Japanese armour as it was for the Japanese sword. The *samurai*, or military class, were firmly established, increased in numbers and powers, and extended their privileges. Intermittent fighting went on, especially during the first half of the XIVth century, when the cause of the eclipsed Emperors was unsuccessfully championed by the patriots Kusunoki (see plate 3) and Nitta against the power of the Shōguns. The other great military event of the period was the defeat of the attempted Mongol invasion of Japan in 1281, in which the

Mongol fleet, like its western counterpart the Spanish Armada, was largely destroyed by a storm.

Fighting on horseback was now on the decline; armour became lighter in consequence, and the gap between *ōyoroi* and *haramaki* was closed by the wearing of helmets and shoulder-pieces with the latter. At the same time certain additions were made to the *ōyoroi*; greaves, first introduced about the XIth century, and a sort of armoured apron under the tassets to give additional protection to the thighs were generally adopted, and the face and neck were covered with an iron mask, often of ferocious aspect, and a laced gorget. Some form of horns and forecrest on the helmet became almost universal, and the bearskin boots of the earlier mounted warriors gave place to more practical sandals. Mail was used to protect the forearms.

The XVth and XVIth centuries are marked by the rise to prominence of the great families of hereditary armourers, chief among whom are the Myōchin and their offshoots the Saotome. The former traced their origin back to the Prime Minister of the Empress Jingō, who is recorded to have invaded Korea at the beginning of the IIIrd century; but they only became strictly historical with Munesuke, who is said to have been given the family name of Myōchin by the Emperor Konoye about the middle of the XIIth century, the family name before this being Masuda. Munesuke is the maker of the helmet-crown of the Akita armour referred to above. It was during the XVth and XVIth centuries also that the use of family badges (*mon*) became very general, and they are a frequent motive in the decoration of armour.

The XVIth century was a time of almost continuous civil wars in which firearms, introduced by the Portuguese, began to play a part. One of the pioneers of the new weapon was Takeda Shingen, a redoubtable warrior-monk, whose ten-year struggle with his neighbour Uyesugi Kenshin between 1553 and 1563 has given artists and romancers many an inspiration. Foreign influence on armour was not extensive, but a number of examples of strong plated cuirasses, inspired by European models, and helmets with a brim, somewhat resembling a cabasset, have survived. Warriors of high rank at this time often wore helmets of freakish design, but common soldiers had to be content with the lacquered leather war-hat or *jingasa*.

During the peaceful seclusion of the Tokugawa rule between 1600 and 1868 armour became progressively less practical and more ornamental. At first armourers concentrated on making it bullet-proof, but once peace was firmly established, they occupied themselves in luxurious adornment and imitations of ancient armour. The disturbances which heralded the Meiji Restoration of 1868 were the last occasion when Japanese armour was worn in battle, and suits made at this time are often largely of cow-hide, tough, light, and practical.

## THE BOW

As has already been noted, the bow was in use in Japan from the earliest times, being at first the chief weapon of the mounted knight. Examples in the Shōsō-in Repository, dating from the VIIIth century, are of various woods, and their lengths vary between about 5 ft. 6 in. and 7 ft. Several of the most noteworthy figures of the mediaeval wars were noted for their skill in archery, especially the giant Tametomo (1139–1170) who used a bow 8 ft. 9 in. in length, and is reported on one occasion to have sunk a boat with a single heavy arrow. Another was Nasu no Yoichi Munetaka, whose descendant Nasu Munemitsu was teaching and practising archery in Kyōto as late as 1937. At the battle of Yashima (1185) the Taira set up a fan on a bamboo pole in the bows of one of their boats as a challenge to the Minamoto; Yoichi, as the best archer among the latter, was ordered to shoot it down. He did so, his arrow striking full on the fan's rivet at a range of nearly a hundred yards.

The normal Japanese bow averages about 6 ft. 5 in. in length, and, like most oriental bows, is of composite construction. A cross-section will reveal that between two thin strips of bamboo forming the "back" and "belly" of the bow are set three further strips of bamboo somewhat thicker than the outer ones and set edgewise to give greater strength; outside these, forming the outer edges of the bow, are two strips of *haze* wood (*Rhus succedanea*), the whole being secured with fish-glue, lacquered over, and bound at intervals with rattan. The grip of deerskin is nearly two-thirds of the way down the bow, and the string is of glass fibre. The bow is drawn well behind the ear, and Japanese arrows are consequently of much greater length than the European type. Examples of the main types of arrow-head can be seen on plate 23.

## POLE-ARMS

The earliest Japanese spears preserved to us, known as *hoko*, go back to the time of the Emperor Shōmu (724–749). The blades are plain and straight, but some are provided with a single hook-like projection at the base. Unlike later examples, which have narrow tangs let into the shaft and secured by a peg like the sword-blade, these early spear-heads are made with hollow sockets. The spear, however, seems to have passed out of use during the early mediaeval period.

But during the Kamakura period the formidable glaive (*naginata*—see plate 22) with its long curved blade, was extensively used, especially on foot, and is thought to have occasioned certain improvements in the armour of the time, such as the introduction of the protective "apron" below the tassets. The wars of the XVIth century saw a revival of the use of the spear (*yari*) whose straight double-edged blade with central ridge was occasionally replaced by a dirk-blade; alternatively spear-heads are sometimes found mounted as daggers. Limited variations in the form of the spear-head are encountered, the commonest of which is the cross-shape (plate 23) and the light halberd (plate 22) in the use of which women of the *samurai* class were sometimes trained.

Pole-arms in the form of hooks, rakes, barbed T-shapes, and a number of others, were used in sea-fights and by the police; but their use was so limited and examples are so infrequent that they only call for a passing mention.

## FIREARMS

The use of firearms was introduced into Japan by the Portuguese in 1543, and the form of weapon then adopted continued almost unchanged up to the middle of the XIXth century. The Japanese never used the wheel-lock, snaphaunce, or flint-lock, and passed straight from the match-lock to percussion and pin-fire. With their usual skill at improving and adapting their models, however, they brought the primitive match-lock to as near mechanical perfection as was possible, whilst their gun-barrels, though generally of heavy type, are of a quality comparable to the best productions of the Persian gunsmiths. They are often adorned with damascening and incrustation of various metals, and many bear the signature of the maker.

But the impression remains that the Japanese never really regarded the use of firearms in war as quite sporting, or consistent with the *samurai* code; also, they were introduced on the eve of the peaceful Tokugawa régime; and it may well be that these considerations prevented their development along the lines followed in Europe. For the Japanese must have known of the newer types of mechanism from the Dutch at Nagasaki and an accurate drawing of a flint-lock pocket-pistol is to be found among the works of Hokusai. But though in general use for hunting, it was only in the Kawanakajima campaigns (1553–1563) between the rival war-lords Takeda Shingen and Uyesugi Kenshin that firearms played a very prominent part in warfare (see plates 2 and 26).

The cannon illustrated (plate 25) are of comparatively small size, the largest being only just over 3 ft. in length; the quality of the bronze-founding is excellent, as might be expected. But large pieces were occasionally used against castles and fortresses, somewhat resembling (if we may trust Japanese illustrations) the monsters used by Sultan Muhammad II against the walls of Constantinople in 1453.

Nevertheless the bow and arrow maintained their position until the middle of the XIXth century. When the Forty-seven Rōnin had entered the palace of their enemy Kōdzuke no Suke to carry out their revenge on the night of January 30th 1703, their leader posted men on the roof to pick off anybody attempting to obtain help from outside. These men were armed, not with guns, but with bows and arrows, with which they carried out their instructions with deadly accuracy.

# LIST OF ILLUSTRATIONS

1. Figure of HONDA TADAKATSU (1548–1610), made for the Boys' Festival. M.59–1949

2 & 3. From colour-prints by UTAGAWA KUNIYOSHI (1798–1861). E.10802–1886, E.2210–1925

4. The swordsmith MUNECHIKA (late Xth century), assisted by the Fox-spirit in the form of a woman, forging the blade KO-GITSUNE MARU ("Little Fox"). Original drawing by KUNIYOSHI, about 1835. E.2250–1909

5. Slung-sword (*tachi*) on stand. M.139–1929

6. Three slung-swords (*tachi*); (i) and (iii) for court wear; (ii) for wear with armour. M.144–1915: M.138–1929: M.1081–1927

7. Two pairs of swords (*daishō*) mounted for civilian wear. M.924, 925–1916: M.20, 21–1949

8. Swords and dirks variously mounted for civilian wear. M 17–1947: M.14–1947: M.137–1929; M.926–1916: M.2660–1931

9. Combat between KAMEŌ MARU (r.) and ARIŌ MARU (l.). Colour-print by KUNIYOSHI, about 1845. E.10930–1886

10. Blades of the *Kotō* period (before 1600).

(i) MASAMUNE (of SAGAMI; 1264–1343). M.20–1912
(ii) SUKESADA (of OSAFUNE, BIZEN; XVIth century). 607–1908
(iii) SADAMUNE (of SAGAMI; 1298–1349). M.935–1916
(iv) HŌJU (of MUTSU; dated 1400). M.16–1947
(v) KANEMICHI (of MINO; XVIth century). M.140–1929
(vi) KUNIMITSU (of TAJIMA; mid XIVth century). M.22–1915
(vii) YASUYUKI (of NAMINOHIRA, SATSUMA; XIVth century). M.357–1940
(viii) MURAMASA (of KUWANA, ISE; XVth century). M.340–1940

11. Tangs and points of *Kotō* blades.

(i) KUNIMUNE (of BIZEN and SAGAMI; 1177–1270). M.21–1915
(ii) SADAMUNE (HŌSHŌ, of YAMATO; early XIVth century). M.23–1915
(iii) KAGEMITSU (of OSAFUNE, BIZEN; XIVth century). M.85–1933
(iv) KANEMOTO (of SEKI, MINO; early XVIth century). M.28–1912

12. Blades of the *shintō* period (after 1600).

(i) MYŌJU (UMETADA, of KYŌTO; 1558–1632). M.21–1912

(ii) HANKEI (NODA, of YEDO; d. 1646). M.6–1947

(iii) SHINKAI (INOUYE, of ŌSAKA; dated 1673). 643–1908

(iv) MASAHIDE (KAWABE SUISHINSHI, of YEDO; 1750–1825). M.3–1932

(v) NOBUKUNI (of CHIKUZEN; dated 1713). M.31–1912

(vi) YASUTSUGU (of ECHIZEN and YEDO; early XVIIth century). M.24–1912

(vii) SUKEMASA (of BIZEN; dated 1922). M.191–1935

(viii) MASAYOSHI (HŌKI NO KAMI, of SATSUMA; dated 1806). 601–1908

13. Tangs and points of *Shintō* blades.

(i) MYŌJU (UMETADA, of KYŌTO; dated 1632). M.5–1947

(ii) YOSHIMICHI (TAMBA NO KAMI, of ŌSAKA; XVIIth century). M.924–1916

(iii) KUNITERU (KOBAYASHI, of ŌSAKA; late XVIIth century). M.926–1916

(iv) MASAYOSHI (TAIRA NO, of SATSUMA; dated 1784). 602–1908

14. Iron Guards

(i) Unsigned early type. Toadstools and young bracken. M.211–1921

(ii) NAKAI TOMOTSUNE of HAGI in NAGATO (1706–1780). Landscape. M.116–1911

15. Sword-furniture of the Gotō school.

(i) Guard; SOKUJŌ (1600–1631). Chrysanthemums and daisies. M.330–1921

(ii) Guard; MITSUMASA (JUJŌ, 1695–1742). The rival generals, TAKATSUNA and KAGESUYE, at the UJI river. M.79–1919

(iii) *Kodzuka* (blade signed by SUKEHIRO 1635–1682) and *Kōgai;* MITSUYUKI (TOJŌ, 1790–1862). Lilies. M.336, 336a–1916

16. Sword-furniture of various schools.

(i) *Kodzuka;* ISHIGURO MASATSUNE I (1760–1829). Goats. M.515–1916

(ii) *Kodzuka;* HIGO style, unsigned. Paulownia badges. M.19–1936

(iii) Guard; KAGA style, unsigned. Willow and Plum-tree. M.28–1920

(iv) Guard; TENKŌDŌ HIDEKUNI (1825–1891). Cat attacked by rats. M.288–1920

(v) *Fuchi-Kashira;* TAKASE HIDENAGA (early XIXth century) TAWARA TŌDA HIDESATO and the bell of MIIDERA. M.1336–1931

17. Sword-furniture of various schools.

(i) *Kodzuka* and guard; unsigned. The Foxes' Wedding. M.33, 34–1920

(ii) *Fuchi-Kashira;* ISHIGURO MASAMICHI (early XIXth century). Fowls. M.1419–1931

(iii) *Kodzuka;* IWAMOTO KONKWAN (1744–1801). The Fox-witch. M.1488–1931

(iv) *Kodzuka;* KAGA style, unsigned. A clump of bamboos. M.531–1911

(v) Guard: IWAMOTO KONKWAN (1744–1801). Monkeys and persimmon. 1438–1888

18. Suit of armour in the style of the KAMAKURA period. M.72–1928

19. The DOI armour. M.130–1914

20. Nine stages in the putting on of armour.
Colour print by GO-UN SADAHIDE, 1853. E.12177–1886

21. Types of Japanese helmets. M.73–1928: 500–1872: M.59–1922: M.611–1911

22. Various weapons and accoutrements.

(i) Two throwing-arrows. M.386–1912: M.1440–1926

(ii) Riding-whip. 361–1865

(iii) Quiver of arrows. M.1118–1926

(iv) Glaive (*naginata*). 258–1865

(v) Two small halberds, probably for women. M.62–1922: M.63–1922

(vi) Pair of bows and quiver mounted for travelling. M.31–1922

23. Spear and arrow-heads of various types. M.384–1926: M.32–1937: M.12–1909: M.945–1916: M.28–1915: M.10–1909: M.96–1919: M.19–1909: M.27–1916

24. Pistols and matchlock guns.
M.482–1911: M.367–1923: M.243–1912: M.121–1922: 450–1883

25. Three cannon and a mortar. 1027a, b, c, d–1871

26. The explosion of a land-mine at the battle of KAWANAKAJIMA (mid XVIth century). Colour-print by KUNIYOSHI, about 1850. E.10723–1886

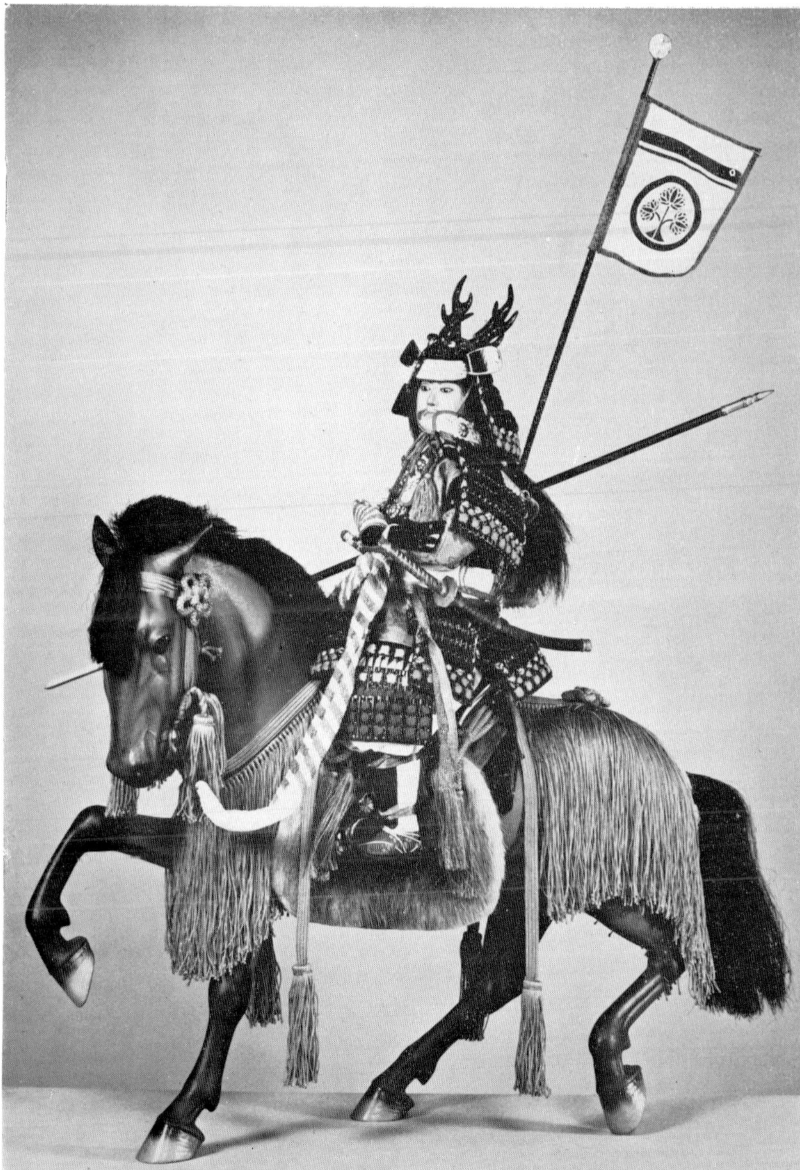

1. Figure of Honda Tadakatsu (1548–1610).

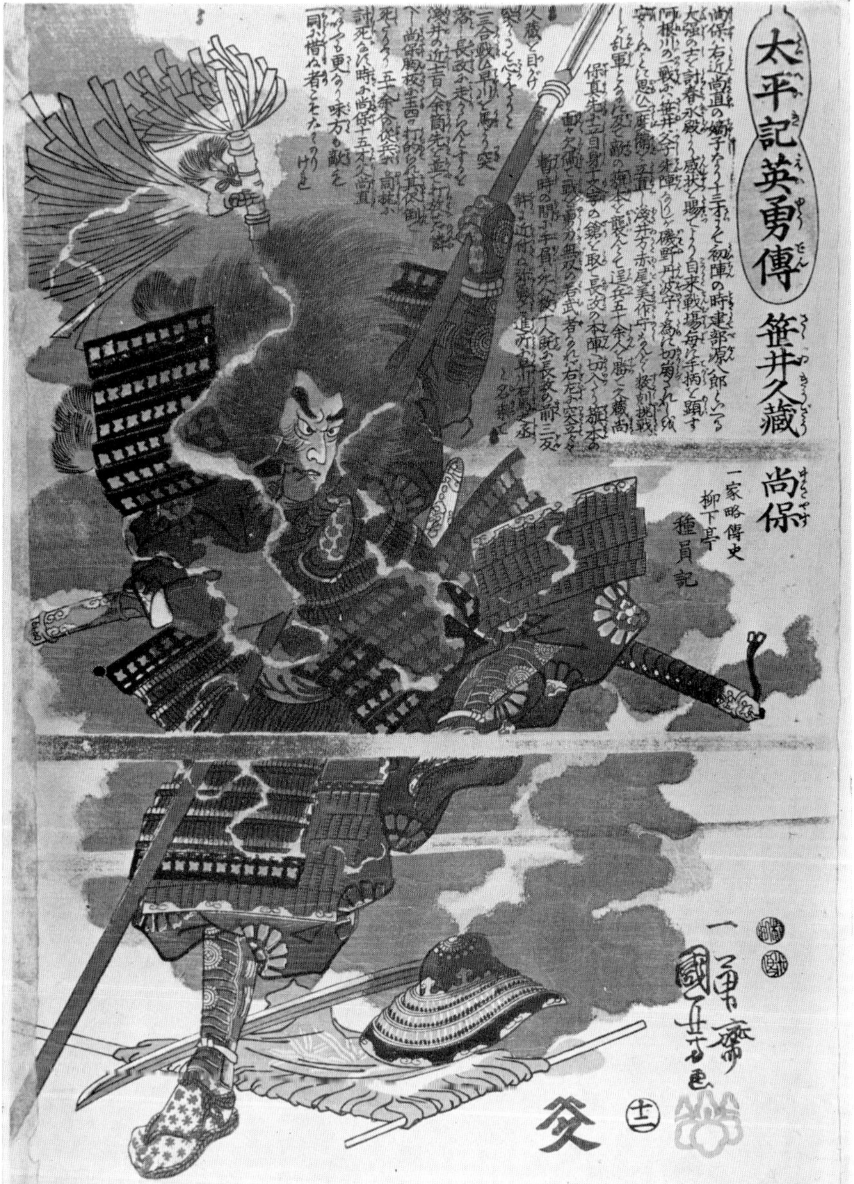


2. Spearman against musketry. By Kuniyoshi.

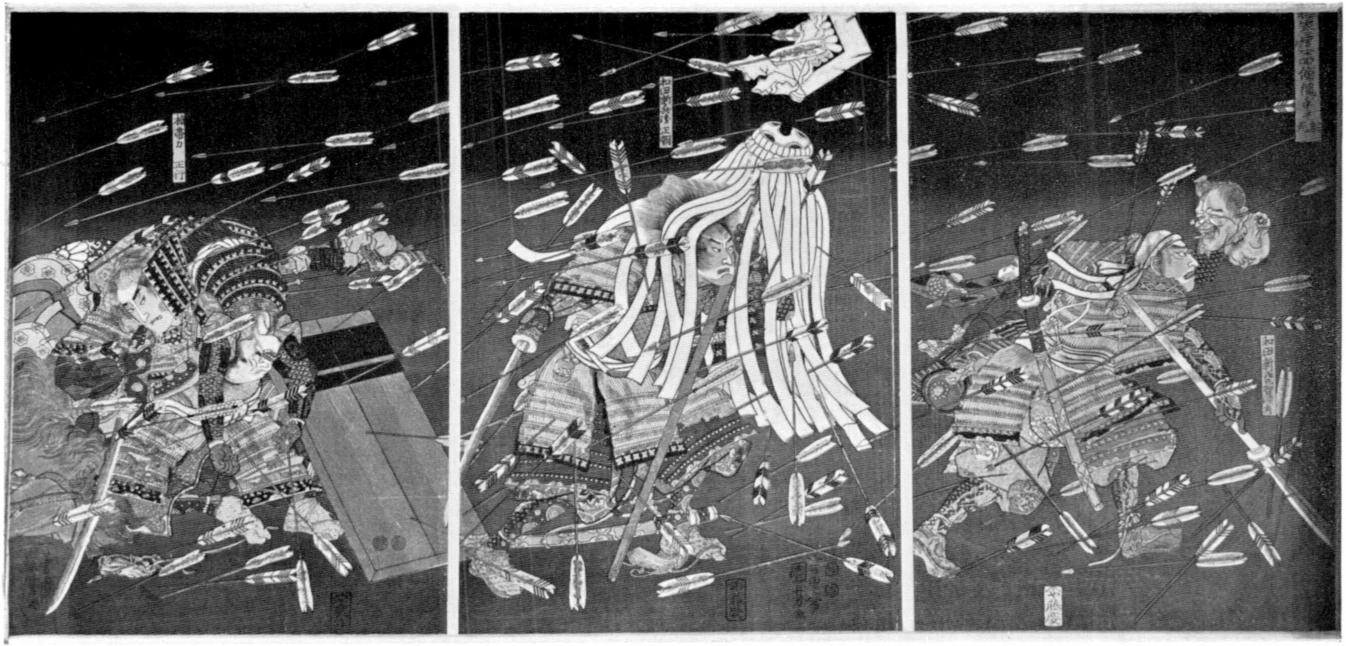

3. Last stand of the Kusunoki clan at Shijō Nawate, 1348. By Kuniyoshi.

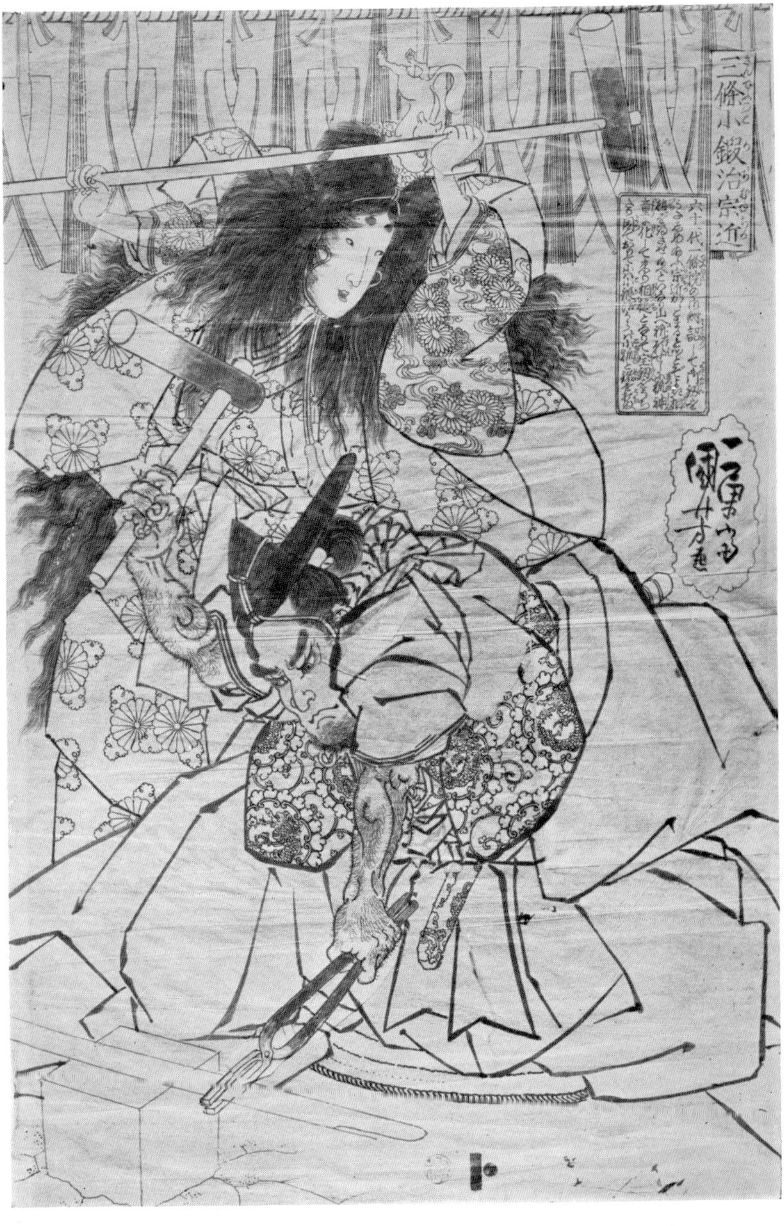


4. Munechika forging the blade "Little Fox". By Kuniyoshi.

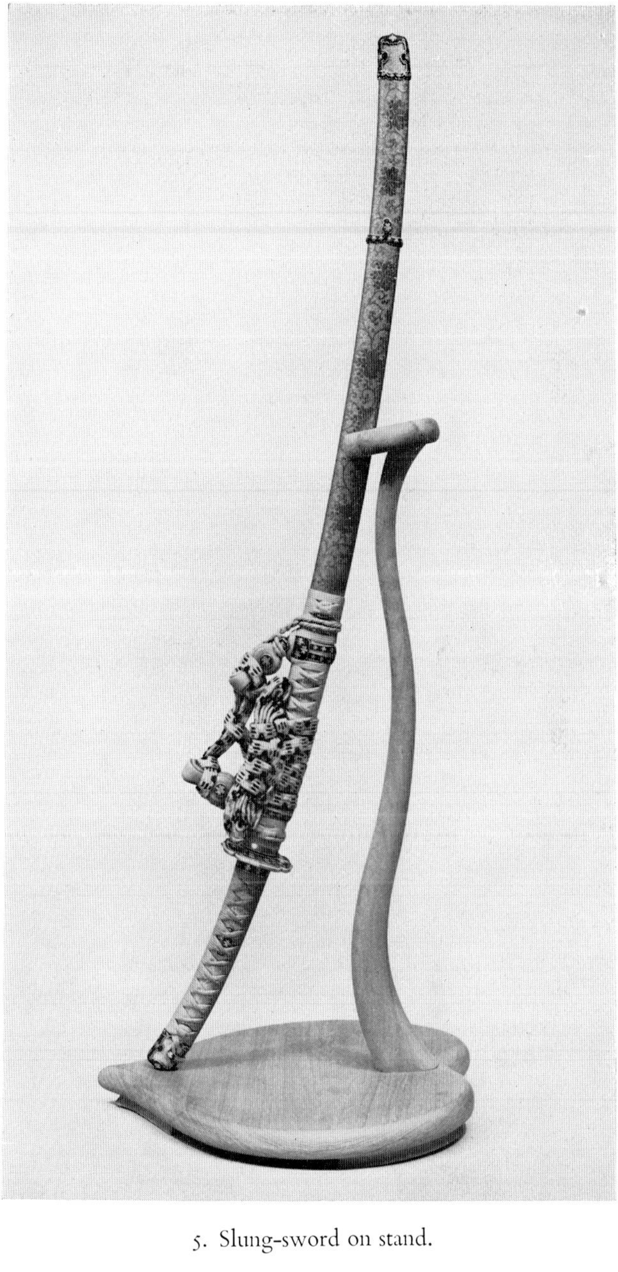

5. Slung-sword on stand.

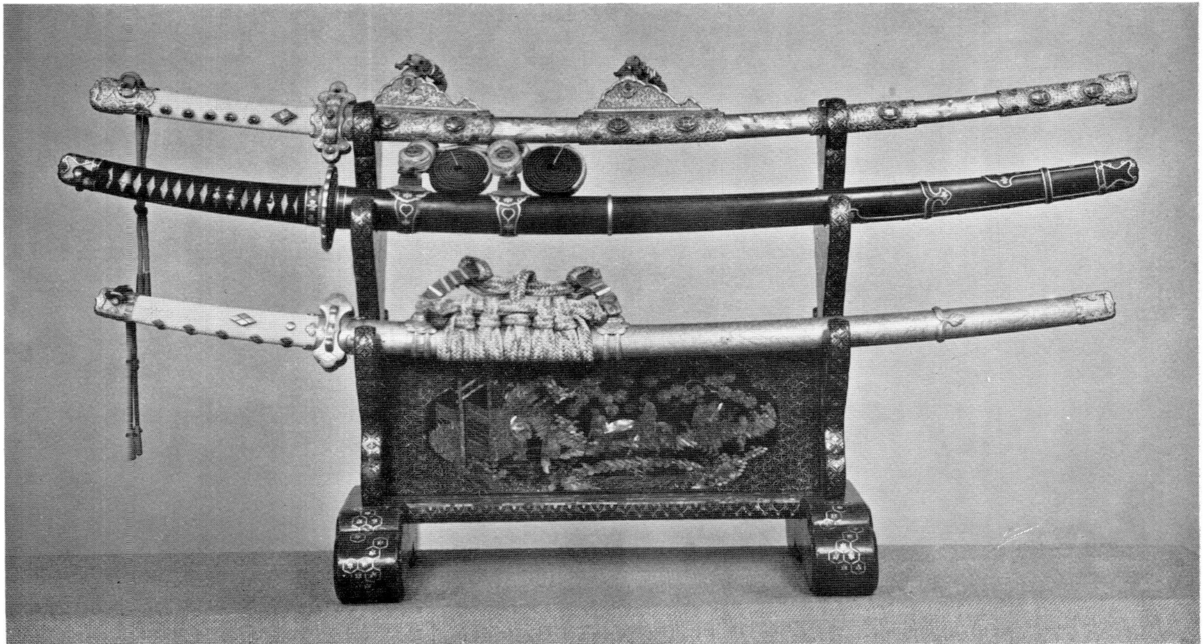

6. Three slung-swords on a sword-rack.

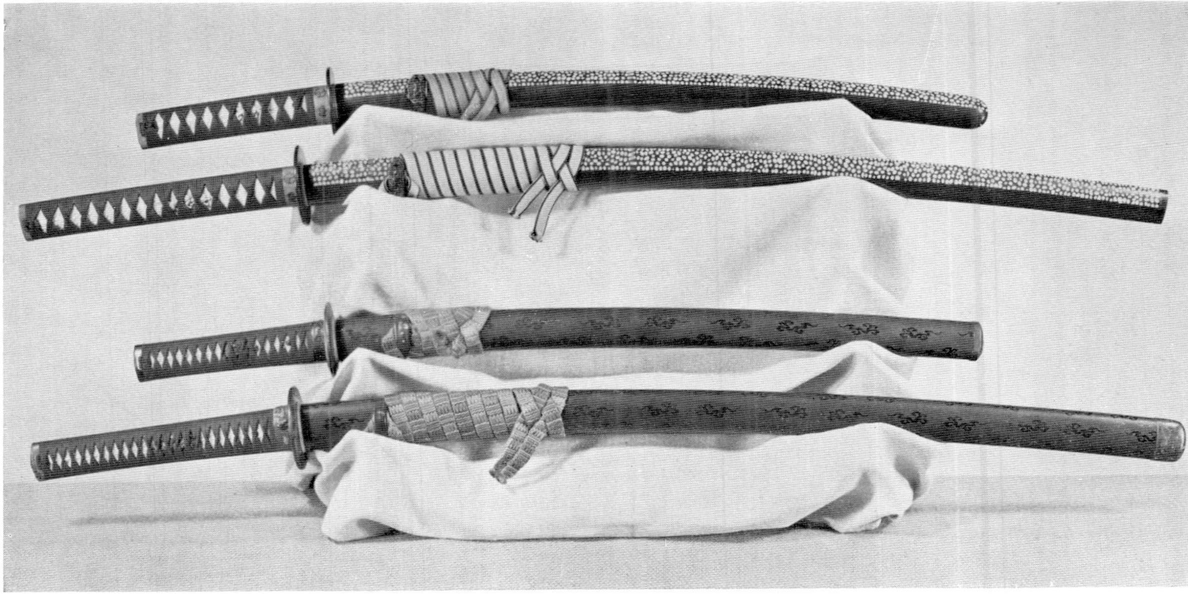

7. Two pairs of swords for civilian wear.

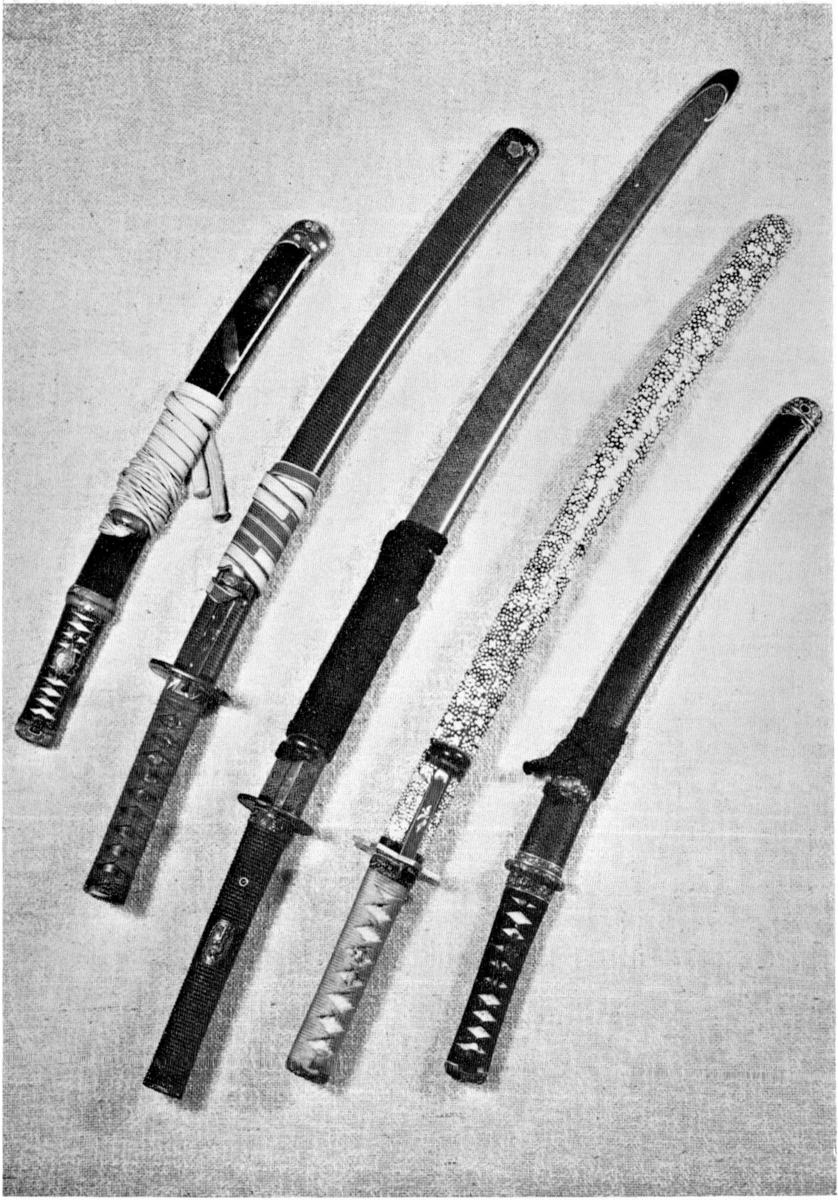

8. Swords and dirks variously mounted.

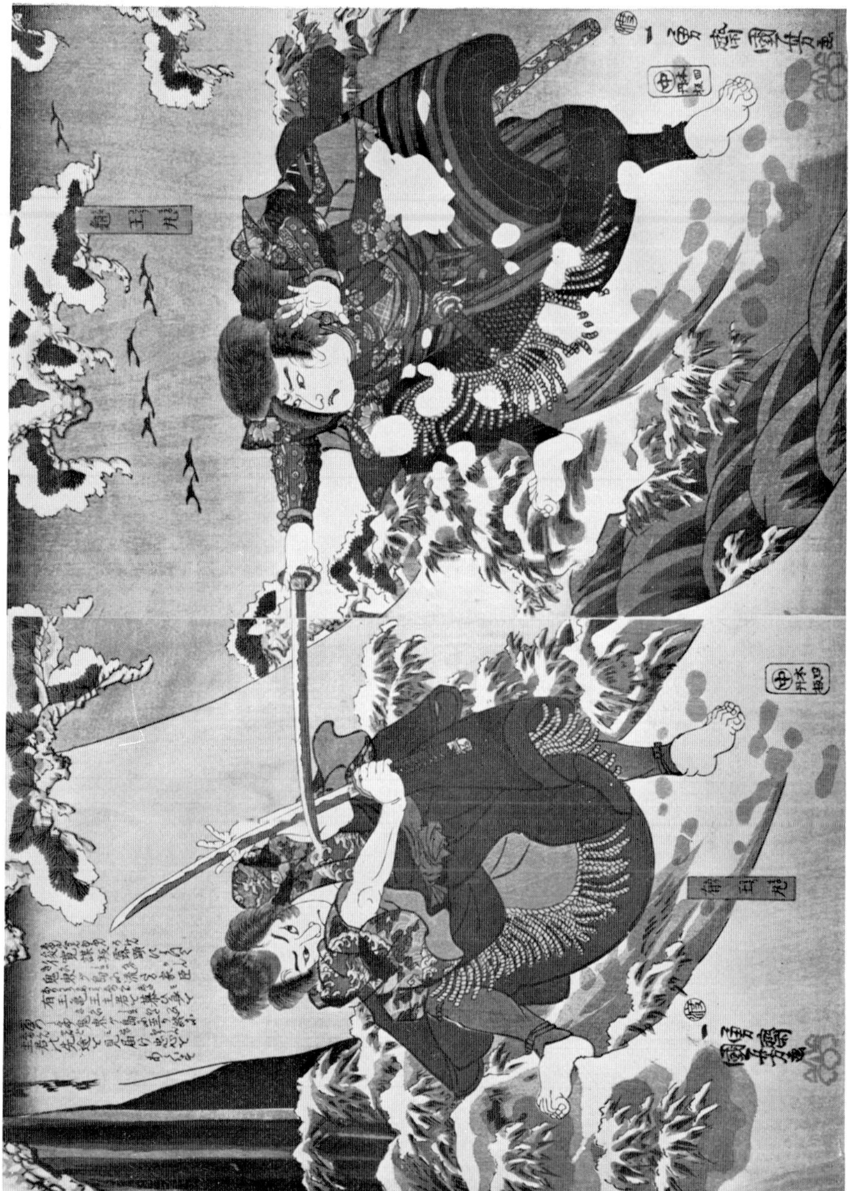

9. Japanese sword-play. By Kuniyoshi.

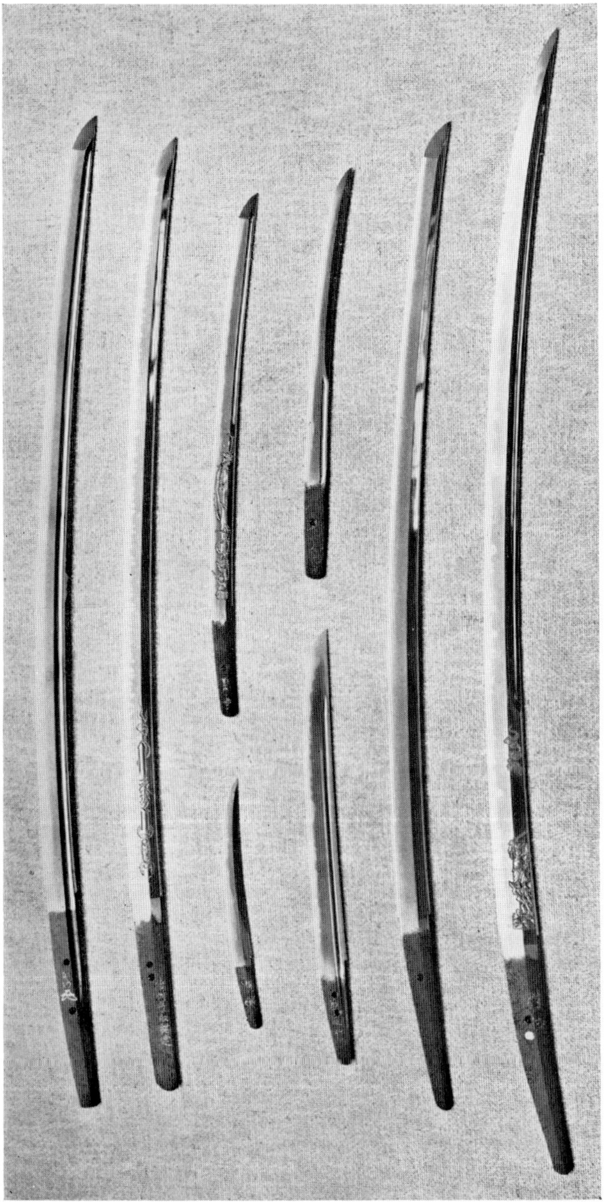

10. Blades of the *kotō* period (before 1600).

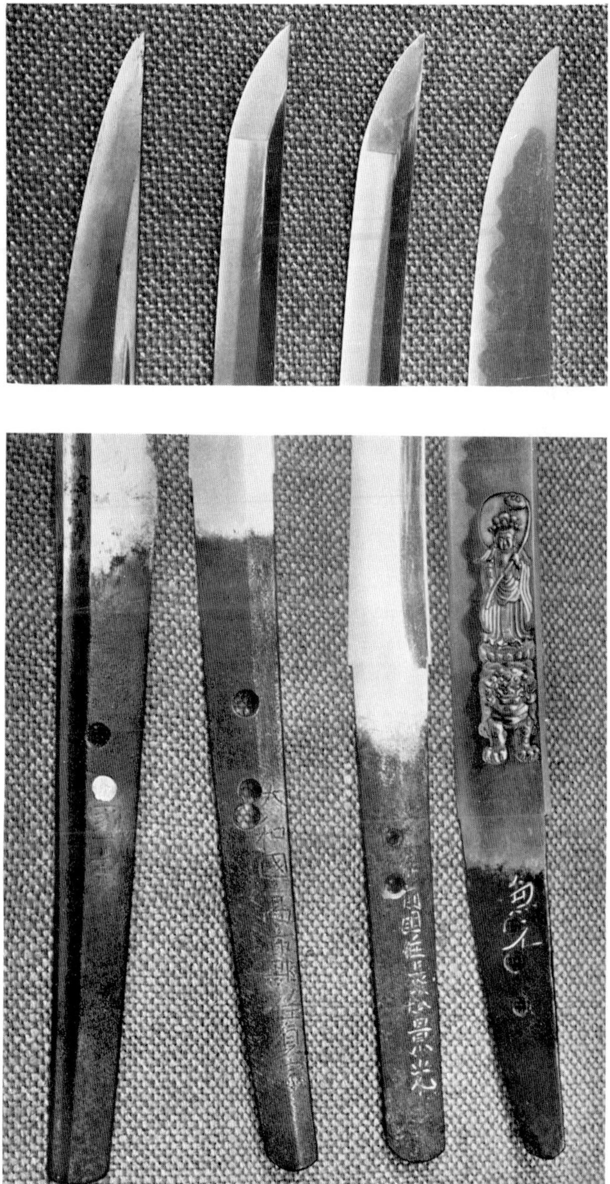

11. Tangs and points of *kotō* blades.

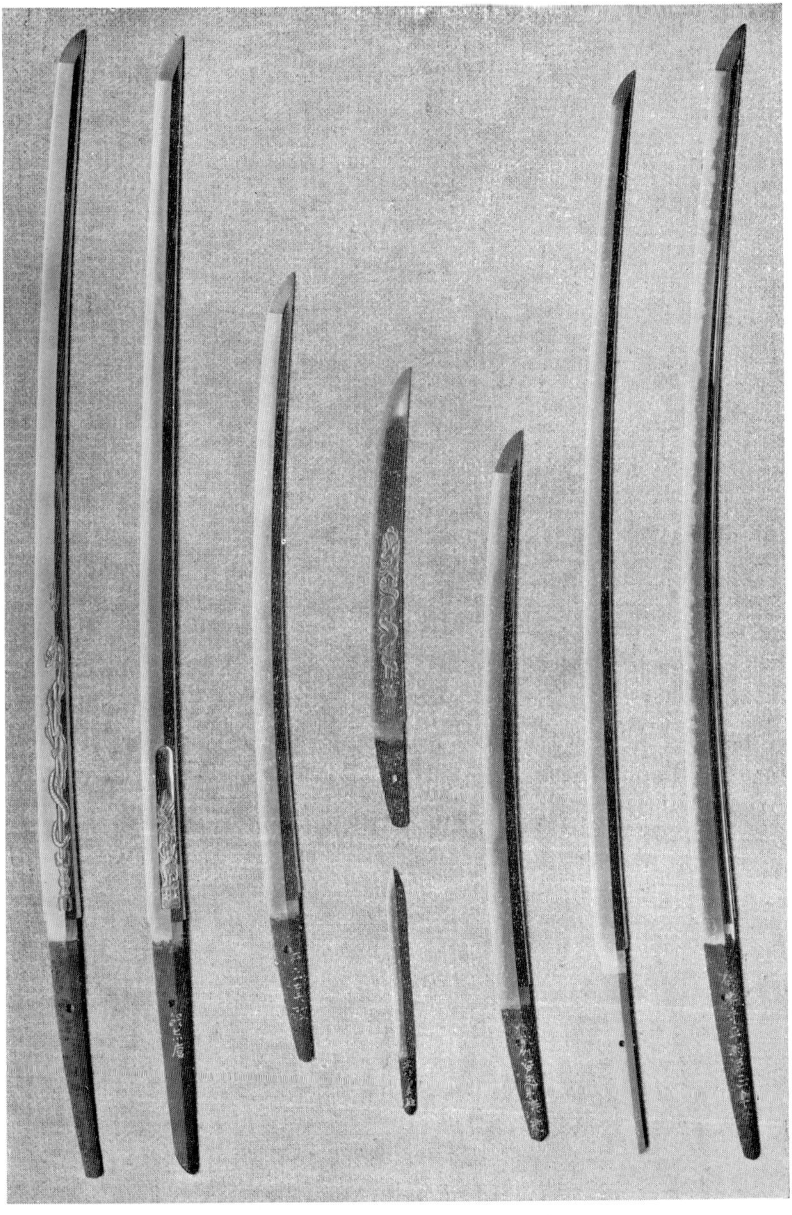

12. Blades of the *shintō* period (after 1600).

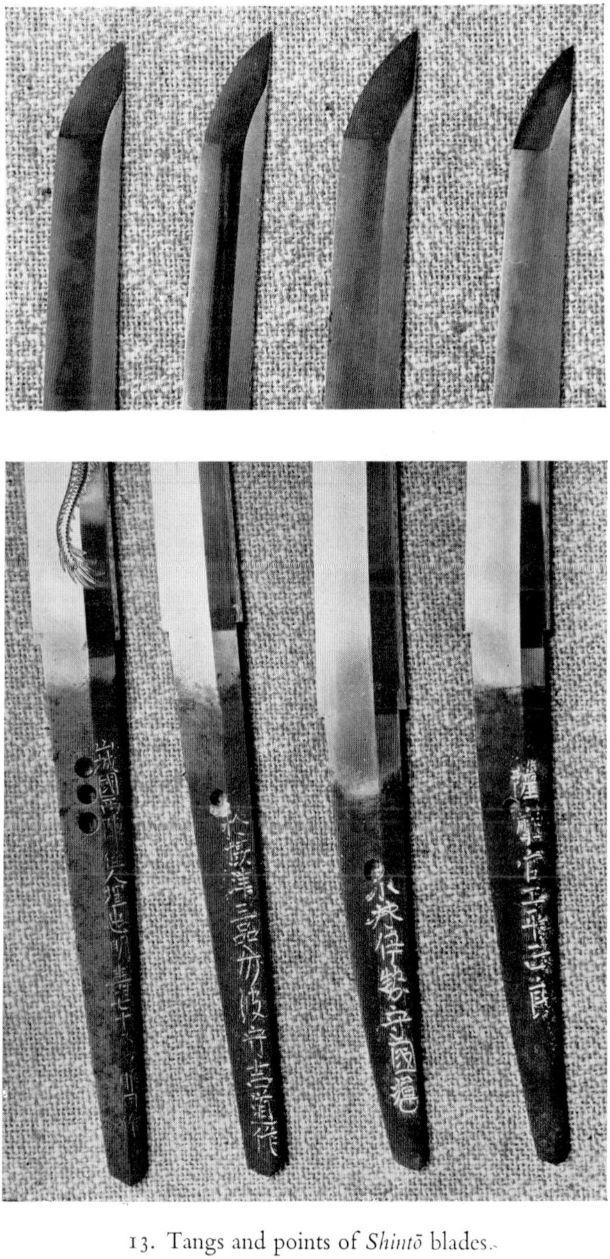

13. Tangs and points of *Shintō* blades.

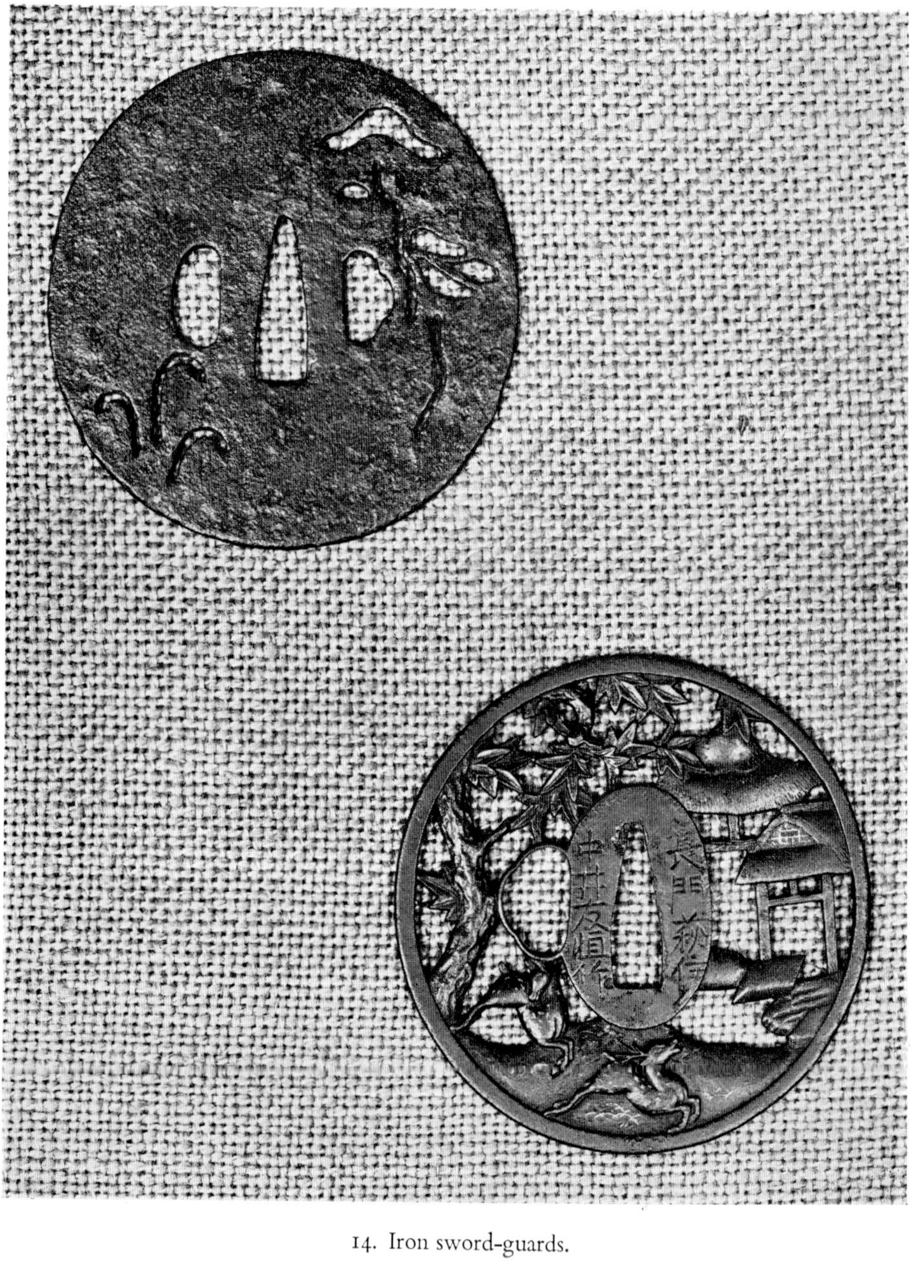

14. Iron sword-guards.

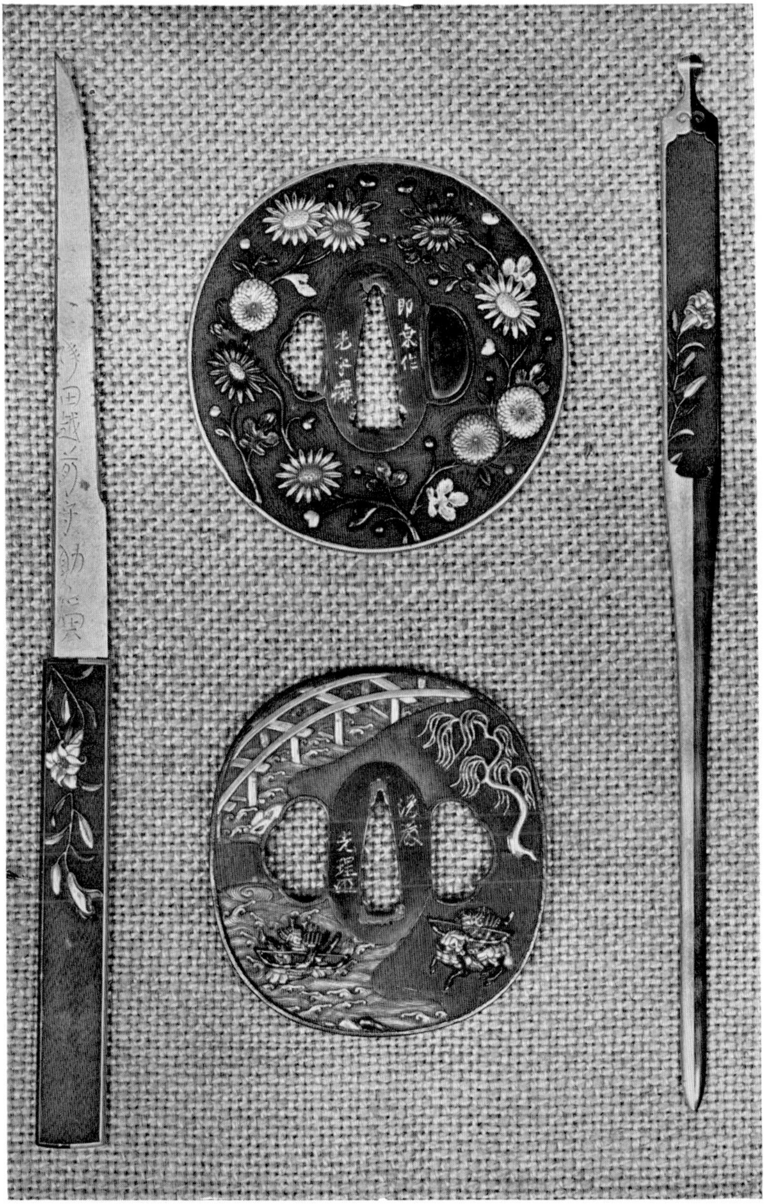

15. Sword-furniture of the Gotō school.

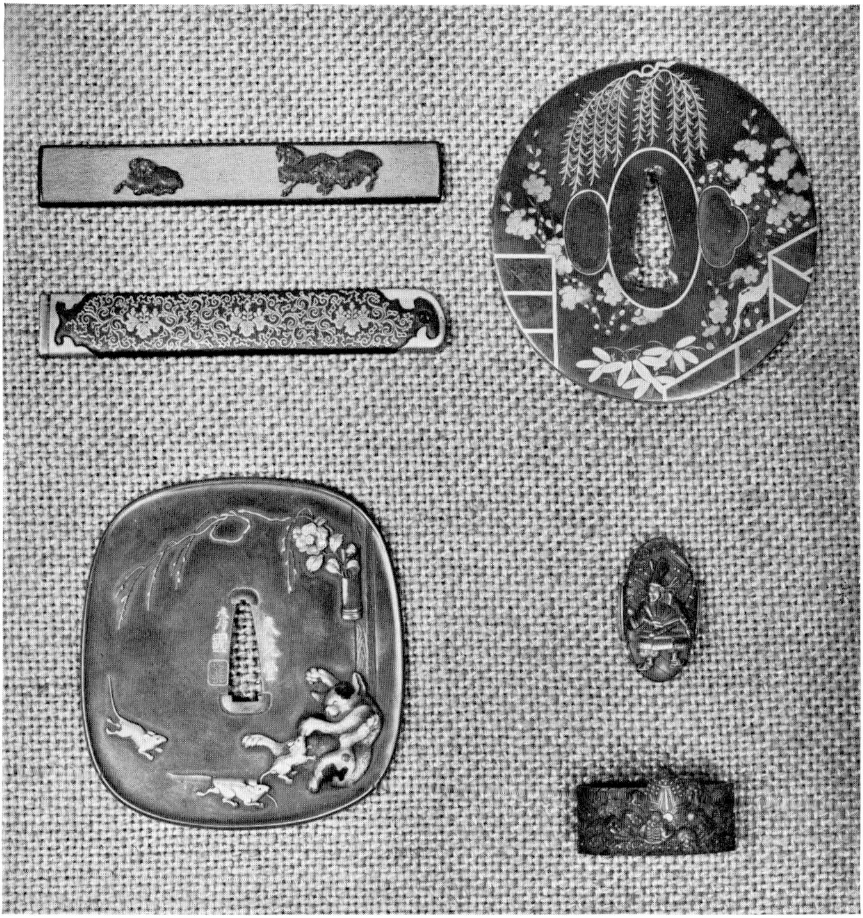

16. Sword-furniture of various schools.

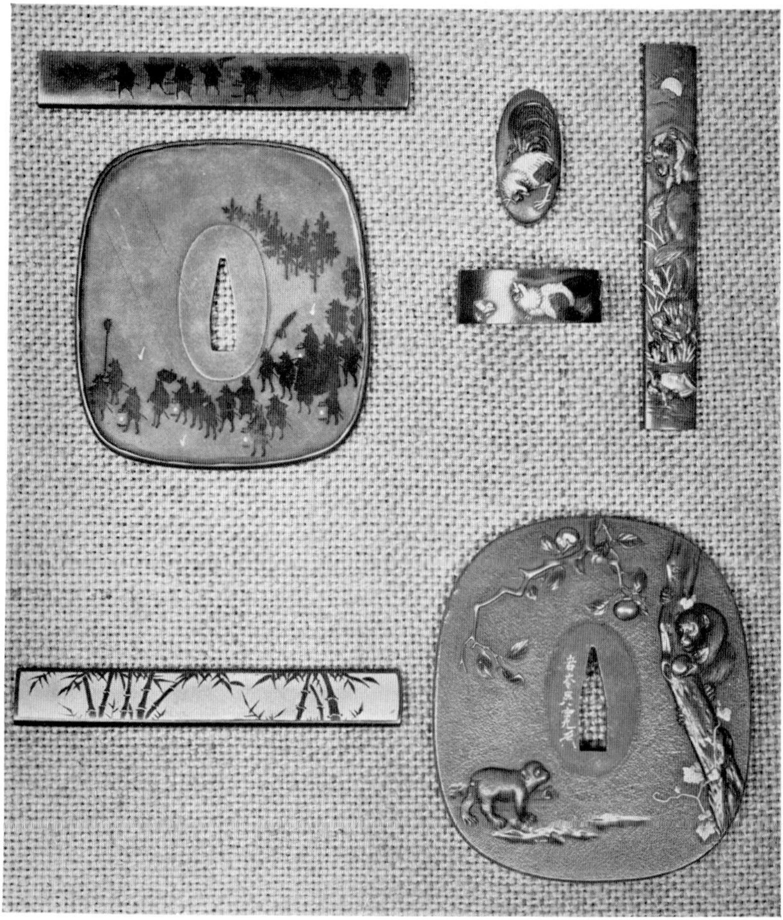

17. Sword-furniture of various schools.

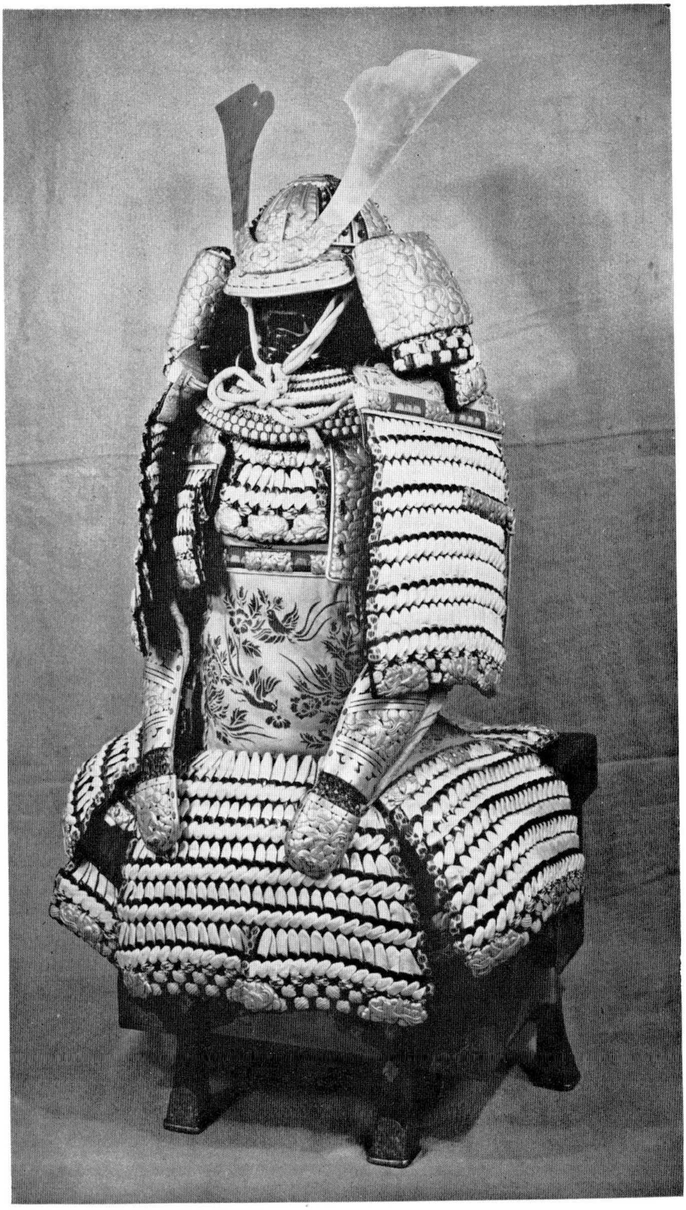

18. Armour of mediaeval style.

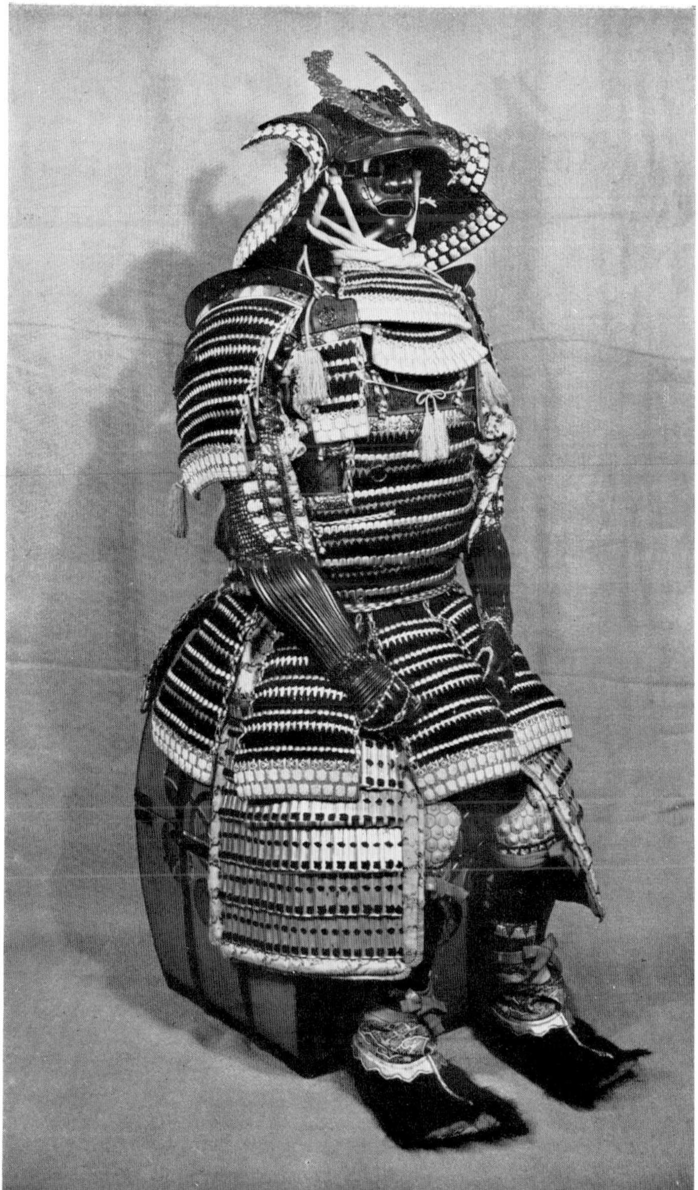

19. The Doi armour.

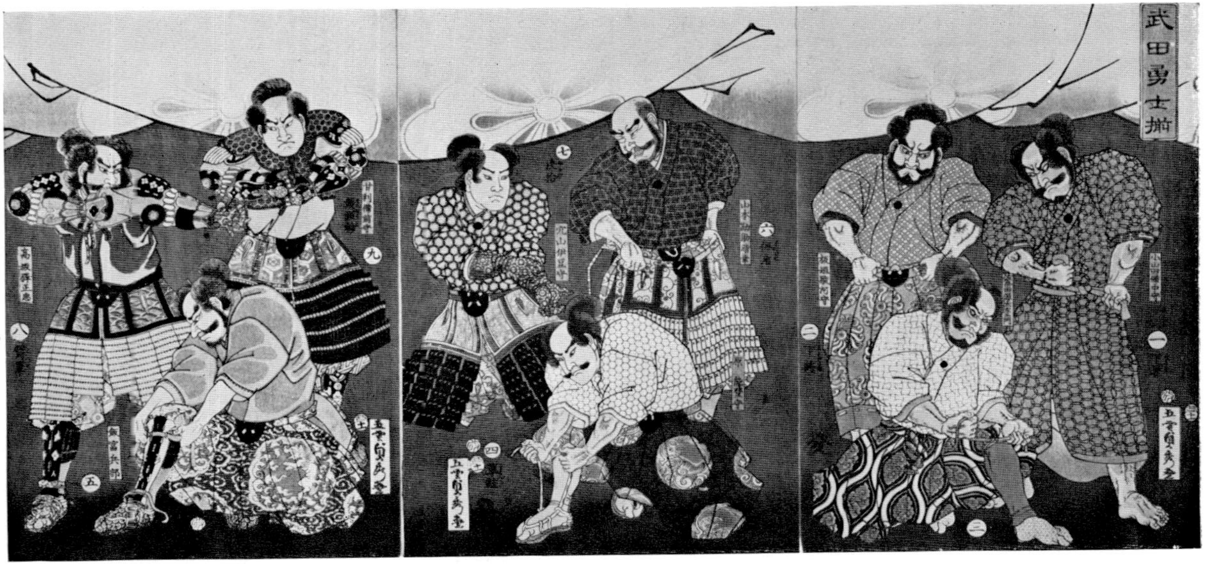


20. Stages of putting on armour. By Sadahide.

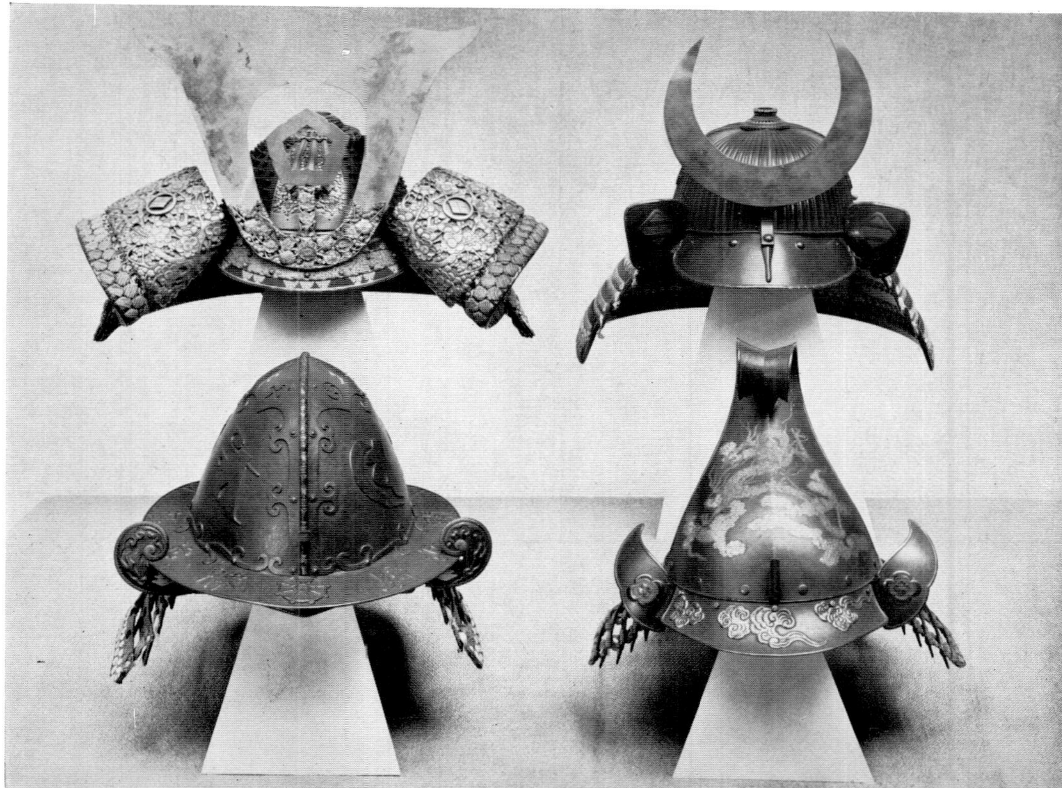

21. Types of Japanese helmets.

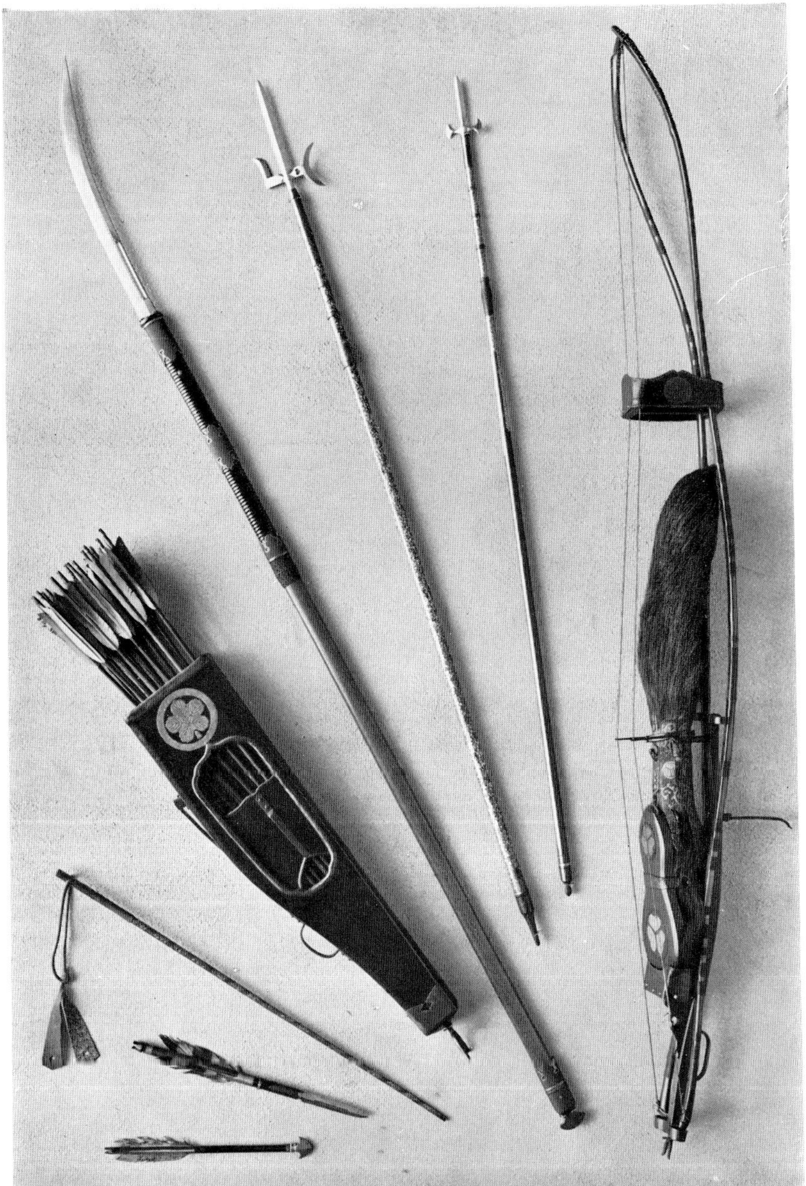

22. Various weapons and accoutrements.

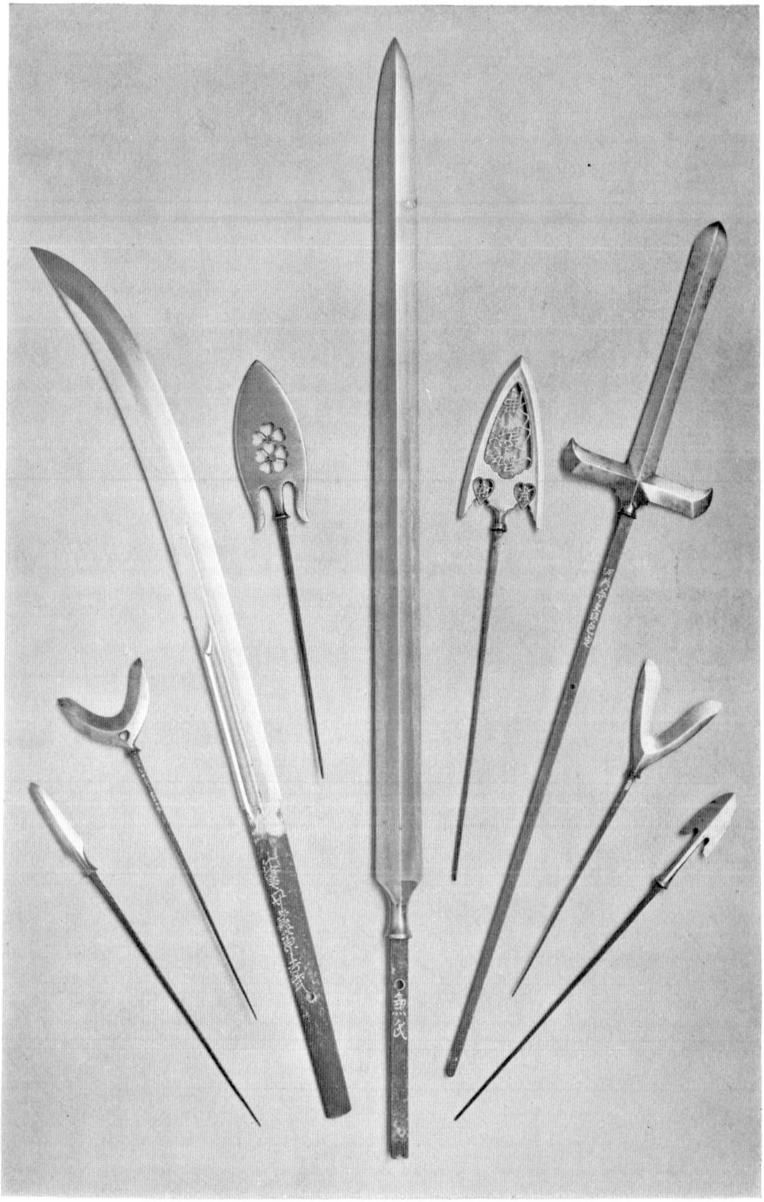

23. Spear and arrow-heads.

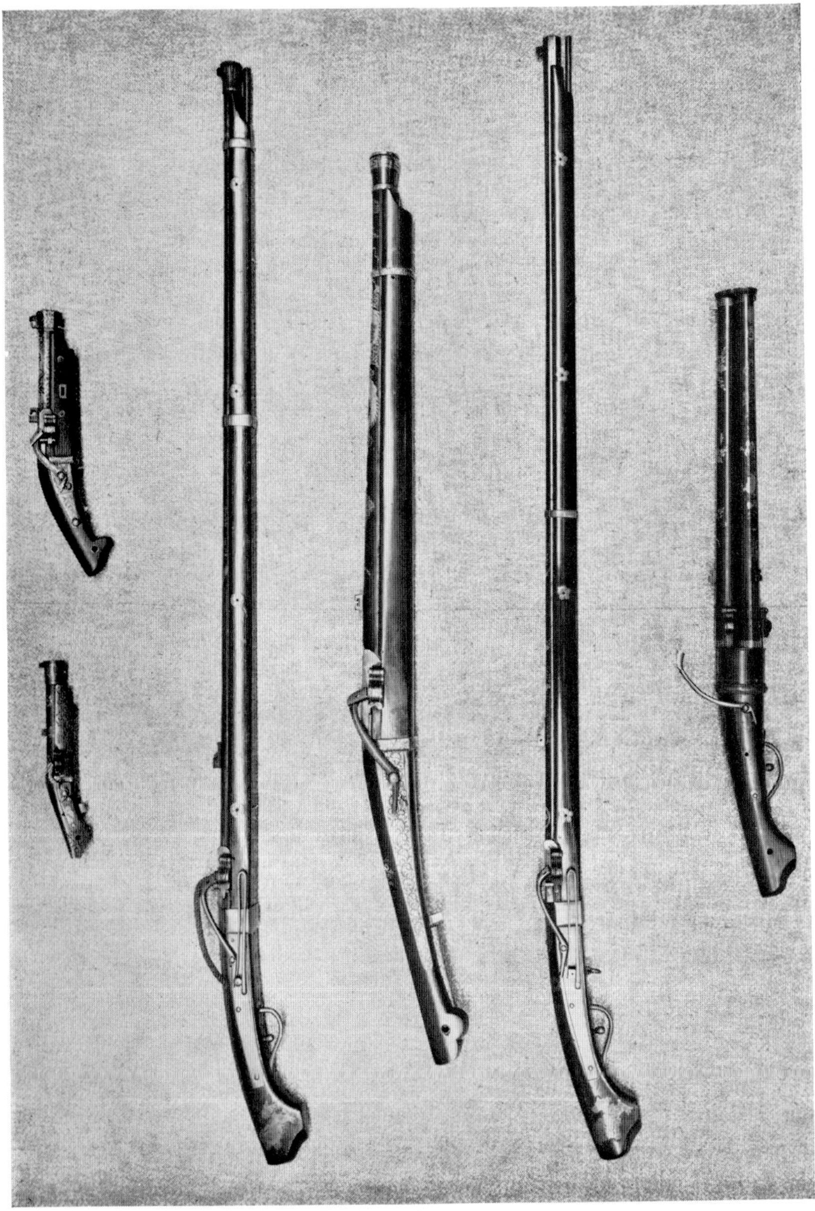

24. Pistols and matchlock guns.

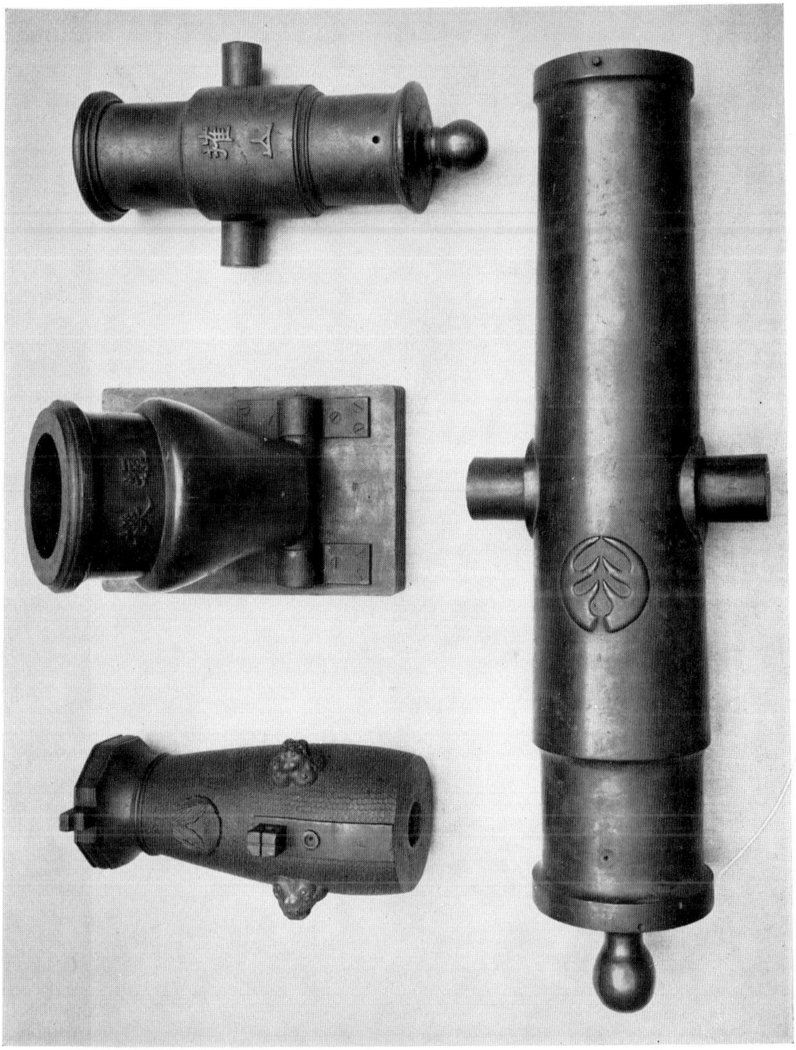

25. Cannon and a mortar.

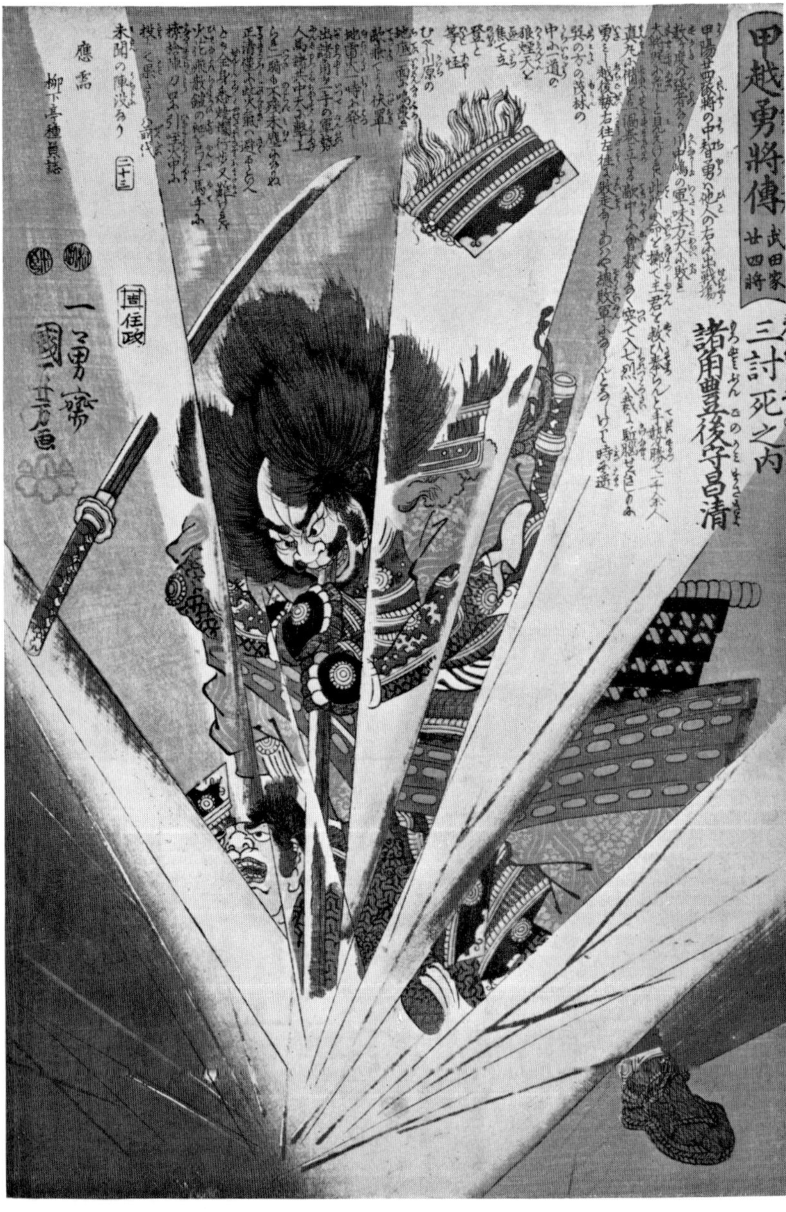


26. Explosion of a land-mine. By Kuniyoshi.

Printed in England for Her Majesty's Stationery Office by
The Campfield Press Ltd., St. Albans Dd. 718101 C40 1/83